CONNEMARA

LEGEND AND
LANDSCAPE

CONNEMARA

LEGEND AND LANDSCAPE

HUGH McELVEEN

N
Nonsuch

'To resist mastery in the present in favour of the freedom of a future we ourselves may never inhabit or recognise.' John Knetchel, *Open City* 1998.

Previous Page: *Reflection at the edge of Connemara.*

First published 2009

Nonsuch Publishing
119 Lower Baggot Street
Dublin 2
Ireland
www.nonsuchireland.com

© Hugh McElveen, 2009

The right of Hugh McElveen to be identified as the Author
of this work has been asserted in accordance with the
Copyrights, Designs and Patents Act 1988.

British Library Cataloguing in Publication Data.
A catalogue record for this book is available from the British Library.

isbn 978 1 84588 952 4

Cover and internal design by Emma Jackson

CONTENTS

The edge of Connemara.

ACKNOWLEDGEMENTS

As with many projects the list of acknowledgements could be longer than the undulating coastline of Connemara. First, a special thanks to my editor Stephanie Boner who initially suggested the book to me. If there was a Nobel Prize for patience it would annually go to editors. Luckily for me Stephanie wields her editorial scalpel with a gentleness in proportion to her patience. Many thanks also to Ronan Colgan at Nonsuch for his enthusiastic support for the project from the off, and to Maeve Convery for her flawless proofreading. If it were not for the Nonsuch trio this book would not exist or would be a case study in flaws. Emma Jackson wove more than a little magic with the design and I am very grateful for her input. All my family, without exception, gave me unconditional and unlimited encouragement. My mother, Kate was with me when I bought my first camera for £8 in 1983 and has given me constant support since then. She lent me many books including a first edition of Lady Wilde's *Ancient Legends of Ireland*. I am very grateful to Denis Hooper, who helped me develop my first role of black-and-white film when I was fourteen and set me a mission with no return. Catherine, my mother-in-law also gave all the help I needed before I could even ask for it, and her home was a springboard to launch me from Galway City into the wonders of Connemara. Dominic, friend and business partner at Exhibit A Studios, shouldered extra work at the studio when I disappeared and was an honest voice to challenge the work I produced. There were many conversations with family and friends that served as stepping stones to new thoughts and you will find echoes of those chats between these covers. Past colleagues and friends from The Gallery of Photography and the Institute of Art, Design and Technology played a huge role in my growth as a photographer and I am forever indebted to them for the oppurtunities they have given me. Thanks are due to all the authors and artists whose work set my mind racing over the last eighteen months. There would never be enough time to read and digest the wealth of information out there. My bookshelf is buckling with future evenings. Participants of the Hugin panoramic software forum showed me how to solve stitching problems. So thanks goes to Bruno, Bart, George, Harry, Andrew and Matthius. Finally, my partner Catherine who humoured my every whim, including buying a VW camper so I could vanish into Connemara for days on end, and provided all the space I needed to work on the images and every encouragement to write the book afterwards. This book is for you, Calum, and Eve with all my love.

Mooring, Lough Corrib. With water borders to the north, east, south and west in the form of Killary Fjord, Lough and River Corrib, Galway Bay and the Atlantic Ocean, Connemara is a virtual island, physically, socially and culturally.

INTRODUCTION

The first problem facing anyone who wants to visit Connemara is to determine exactly where Connemara is. It is not a political or geological region. Possibly the greatest living authority on Connemara is Tim Robinson, a man who has walked the length a breadth of the region to produce a map that transcends being a mere 'how to get to' representation of an area to being a document of his experience of a place. The map of Connemara is informed by long walks and longer conversations with the many people he came across in his cartographical pursuit. The edge of Connemara is a penumbra; its exact position depends on who you ask. Acknowledging this, Robinson has identified the limits of Connemara based on his intimate experience of the region. He has classed three levels of Connemaricity. These are indubitable, arguable and fanciful.[1] This book has chosen to identify the Connemara of this middle ground. Arguable Connemara lies to the West of the line that links Leenaun, Maam, Maam Cross and Spiddal.

The west of Ireland has some of the most spectacular scenery the country has to offer. Nowhere is this as obvious as in Connemara. Here the richness of the landscape is matched by the richness of the culture. In Connemara the Irish language is still strong, although in puddles shrinking under a hot sun. Traditional music and farming practice continue to thrive in this region also. Much of Ireland's folklore has been associated with Connemara and remains an integral part of the local culture. Myles Dillon documented many stories from Galway in the 1930s and compiled some of them into his book *There Was a King in Ireland*. This persistence of Irish heritage did not come about through design, but rather as a result of Connemara's geographical and economic marginalisation through the centuries. The absence of outside inference has served to ensure the traditional lifestyle's endurance.

'Iar' is the Irish word for west. The dictionary on my shelf tells me it can also mean: after, post, late, and end. Words built on 'iar' have a common thread: 'iarbháis' (post-mortem), 'iarchonn' (hindsight), 'iargúil' (backwater), 'iargúlta' (isolated), and so on. This association with loss and defeat has been borne out in events of mythology and history up to the present day. The west was where Goll retreated when chased by Fionn's men, it was where Cromwell's vanquished went and today it is part of the BMW (Border, Midland and West), an area of special government grants, to compensate for economic disadvantage.

'I am the sum total of my ancestor's existence.'[2] This statement of a Maori leader expresses a universal experience. An individual's identity is derived from a sense of a belonging to their people and is defined by a flag, an anthem, culture and traditions. The obsession of ex-patriot communities with the culture of their homeland exemplifies our need for a cultural as well as a unique identity.

Every generation builds on that of its parents. Each generation makes new advances in science, technologies and the understanding of the world. Every age believes itself to have a truth and understands the beliefs of previous generations to be erroneous or legend, which

Derryclare Lough and island is one of Ireland's most photographed and clichéd vistas. Despite its scenic potential the government has threaded telephone cable across it rather than burying them.

we assimilate into our own belief system. As a consequence we mythologise the beliefs of our ancestors. We use the words legend and myth in a derogatory sense to dismiss the ideas and values of our predecessors. In the same way our children will cast aside our understanding of the world and relegate it to fiction.

Just as we can trace our genetic ancestry, we can follow the path of the evolution of our beliefs. Ireland is no different to many other cultures when we discover that our stories and beliefs were born out of the landscape.[3, 4] Aboriginal Australians sang their songlines as they walked through the landscape to neighbouring communities. These songs were a verbal map of a highly articulate culture. Knowing these stories as we walk through the landscape cannot but enrich our enjoyment of it. By understanding our landscape we understand our history and consequentially we understand ourselves.

In Ireland, while the examples are not so obvious, if we dig a little we can find countless occurrences of this profound relationship between legend and landscape. In Connemara, this connection goes back at least as far as the naming of the region. The name Connemara translates as Conn of the Sea, who is associated with the high king Conn of the hundred battles. The land of the dead, the Otherworld, lay beyond the sea and many of the stories are associated with it.

The sunset we see sinking into the Atlantic was the fiery eye of Goll descending into the underworld to meet with Conn in Neolithic times. The Iron-Age fire goddess became St Brigid in the age of Christianity. The Goddess's domain was the hearth above which, her personification, the fire wheel was hung.[5] This fire wheel was appropriated by early missionaries and became her Christian cross, which is still much in evidence throughout Ireland today.

These examples represent the four belief ages of Ireland. Pre-history saw a maternal earth goddess culture in the Stone Age. This grew into a male warrior society during the metal ages. The arrival of Christianity was a fundamental shift of beliefs and societal values which in turn is being replaced by an age of scientific secular rationalism.[6]

Apart from the use of the landscape by indigenous people, colonisers reworked the landscape to remind themselves of the lands they left. These manufactured topographies are now considered vistas of natural wonder. However, they are anything but, and this theme-park-isation of the landscape still continues today in the shape of golf courses and organised recreation.[7] This phenomenon has been observed by many academics. A well-known example of the landscape being moulded by a colonial landlord is Luggalaugh in Co. Wicklow. The La Touche family transported

several thousand tonnes of Brittas Bay sand to the estate so that they could have a silver lakeside shore. This taming of the landscape happened throughout Ireland, and the estates of the West were no exception. Rhododendron is the omnipresent reminder of this desire to manipulate the land. Its very occurrence is an echo of our colonised past, as are rabbits, introduced by the Normans.[8]

Many of the managed estates of yesterday have become the member-only golf courses of today. Both have at their heart the privilege of access and an elite membership. The consequences of this remodelling of the landscape have not all been negative, however, as it has given use to land that was previously too poor to provide a livelihood. The outcome of the impoverished landscape was desertion and the economic migration of its people to foreign urban conurbations. Echoes of this resonate very strongly today as we view the crumbling cottages and new communities in Ireland.

Tír na nÓg also lies to the West and this mythical land of youth from Celtic Mythology became a very real land of opportunity for nineteenth-century immigrants sailing to New York. In the 1950s this desertion continued as the focus switched to London.[9]

Another feature of adaptation by Christianity is the holy wells dotted through the countryside. These have had healing powers associated with them since prehistoric times.[10, 11]

As the poor land failed to provide a living for the many of its citizens when the farm was passed to the eldest son, the Landless became the Diaspora. Still, many of those who remained could not afford to stay and deserted small holdings to seek new lives in other places. The West became dotted with dilapidated homesteads.

Nobody likes to be reminded of their ancestral poverty and as a result, our traditional architecture has been treated with contempt as the countryside has been dotted with aesthetically vacuous bungalows built alongside the ruins of yesterday.[12]

As the pace of our lives and transport gets increasingly faster we have less time for leisure and less time to glance at our surroundings as we shoot through them. This growing disconnect from our heritage is at our peril. Unless we understand the land that made us we will not understand ourselves.

The aim of this book is two-fold. Firstly, it hopes to celebrate the landscape on the extreme, remote west of Ireland and secondly, through its stories and history, to uncover the wealth of information that this terrain contains. In short this book is an attempt to reclaim the cultural richness of Connemara through exploring its landscape.

Road, turf and rhododendron, near Fermoyle.

Domestic standing stones near Carna.

Cottage near Fermoyle. The corrugated roof and doorless opening
suggest the cottage is now being used as a shed or shelter for animals.

Stone barn and gorse in front of cloud covered hills on the road to Clifden.

Cottage and bridge on road to Carna.

Mag Mel translates as 'Plain of Honey'. It is the ribbon of gold cast by the setting sun across the sea. The Mag Mel was the path the pre-Christian dead walked to get to the other world. Roads represent the modern Mag Mel not as a spiritual commute but as a more utilitarian path as commuters and tourists buzz from A to B. As roads become more important than the landscape they cut, they present their own graphic aesthetic.

Modern Mag Mel between Twelve Bens and Errisbeg.

*At the back of Errisbeg facing Toombeola.
Beola was a giant and chieftain. This is
where his tomb lies. The Twelve Bens are
named after Beola.*

At the back of Errisbeg facing Ballinaboy.

Mag Mel was the path pre-Christian spirits walked to get to the Otherworld or Hy-Brâzil. Walking on the water has obvious connotations that the early Christians were able to exploit.

Killary Fjord and Mweelrea Mountains. The skeletons of famine villages can be seen on both sides of the fjord illustrating how densely populated this area once was. Industry has now returned to the fjord in the form of fish farms and tourism.

Previous page:
Cloud, Twelve Bens and coniferous forest.

Gravel.

On the road to Roundstone from Ballynahinch.

At Maam Cross.

Killary walk. Along the Connemara side of the fjord is a path which passes Foher and crosses St Roc's pass.

BEFORE WORDS WERE WRITTEN

The story of Connemara begins, before the arrival of men, with the sculpting of the landscape by the last Ice Age. As the ice retreated it left reminders dotted on the plains. Boulders rising above the horizon stand like sentinels watching the changes through the centuries.[1] During the time of British rule these naturally placed standing stones found a new and subversive function as mass rocks.

Fields peppered with stone are of little use for agriculture and before any farming could take place the glacial debris had to be removed. On the Aran Islands alone there are over 3,000km of stone walls.[2] Sometimes the granite blanket is so dense that to build more walls would be a greater exercise in futility than King Canute asserting his will over the sea. Instead Irish farmers built 'alters' reminiscent of those found in South America and Tenerife. Thankfully, in Connemara they were only associated with sweat and tears, not the blood of their foreign counterparts.

In approximately 10,000 BC man first arrived in Ireland, 13,000 years after the retreat of the last ice. As with other civilisations around the world, the prehistoric Irish sought to explain their observation of various natural phenomena with divine and supernatural events. The east-west esker (eiscir in Irish) links Galway and Dublin. It is on this ridge of glacial deposit that Goll mac Morna fought his last battle with Fionn mac Cumhaill.

GOLL MAC MORNA AND FIONN MAC CUMHAILL

The lives of Goll and Fionn are forever tied by mutual respect and adversity. This entanglement starts before Fionn was born and Goll lost his eye, when he was known as Aed (meaning fire).[3] At the Battle of Cnucha (Castleknock) in the Phoenix Park, Aed slew Fionn's father Cumhall and took his crown. In this same battle his eye was struck out by Luchair (bright) and thereafter he became known as Goll (one-eyed). He then succeeded Cumhall as the leader of the Fianna.[4] Muirne, pregnant with Cumhall's child, fled to a safe place and gave birth to Fionn.[5] Fionn grew up in the east of Ireland to become leader of the Fianna. Despite this, Goll provided constant protection for Fionn when he succeeded him.[6] It was as if he knew his death must happen at Fionn's hand. Therefore Fionn's death before Goll's would result in a prophesy unfulfilled. In this way Goll becomes the true self-sacrificing anti-hero and as such his life has to end with tragedy. After Fionn's ascendency Goll went to the west to become the leader there. Goll saved Fionn from many fates in life, including his captivity by the Three Hags at the Caves of Keshcorran. Upon his release Fionn killed Goll's favourite grandson Fedha (songbird) son of Cainche. Eventually, their tempestuous relationship broke down. Many different reasons are given for the final straw that led to war; one story has it that after many defenceless women and children were burnt to death at Fionn's fortress, Almhú, the final battle on the esker took place.

Standing with Goll's Army. With the sun to his back Goll faced the east and its ascendant warrior Fionn. The defeat of the setting west by the rising east has Christian parallels.

Another attributes the call to war with the death of Goll's wife, who was also Fionn's daughter. Fionn was believed to have been responsible for her death. A third says that Goll reacted to the slight which was inferred when he was not given the champion's portion of roasted pig. Whatever the reason, the opportunity to broker another uneasy peace had passed.

The armies of east and west lined up. The symbolism of the alignment should not be lost. Fionn personified youth, the dawn of a new day rising in the east, while Goll embodied defeat, death and the end of the day. He was represented by the setting sun. It was also symbolism that Christianity could exploit.

His army defeated, the starving and exhausted Goll mac Morna was eventually killed by Fionn on the cliffs of Connaught at Nephin Beg.[7] The weapon Fionn used had been previously given to him by Goll. Mortally wounded, the fiery one-eyed warrior slid down the cliffs into the Atlantic to meet with Conn na Mara (Conn of the sea/Otherworld)[8] in the underworld.

Once more the west accepts the death of a vanquished hero. Goll gave his name to the word 'golighe' (setting of the sun) and so ensured his immortality.

Even in death, Goll came to the aid of Fionn when he descended into hell to rescue Fionn from the 'Demons of the Blue Host'.

LIFE AFTER DEATH

The Otherworld lay beyond the sea off the coast of Connemara. It was known by a variety of names. Tír na nÓg (Land of Youth), Tír Beo (Land of Life), Mag Már (The Great Plain), Tír na Fírinne (Land

of Truth) and Hy-Brâzil are just some of the names this ethereal island was called.

During the nineteenth century, the belief in Hy-Brâzil was so certain that John Purdy gave it co-ordinates on his celebrated Atlantic Chart. For twenty-five years, between 1835 and 1860, it held the position 51°10' north 15°30' west. Visit this co-ordinate and all you will find is water. In the early 1900s a considerable number of Aran islanders still believed that the island appeared on the horizon every seven years.[9]

Seeing as how Christ was not due to be born for another couple of millennia and no one else had figured out the trick of walking across water, the early Irish needed another method to get across the sea to Mag Már. The recognised path was across the Mag Mel (Plain of Honey), which appeared with the setting sun.[10] Honey was one of the most coveted foodstuffs available in prehistoric Ireland. It was the natural sweetener used in cake and it was the principle ingredient in the alcoholic mead. Therefore it is fitting that the chief constituent of celebratory foods should form the path to the celebrations in the other world. The honey poured from the observer and over the ocean's horizon.

It is simplistic to try and connect every aspect of Celtic beliefs to parallels in the natural world, and the academic J.A. MacCulloch strongly argues this point.[11] But on occasion the evidence seems very strong and this tendency has been well documented in other countries, so why should it not hold true in Ireland as well? Michael Dames points out, 'Myth reactivated by human rites also requires a sacred place, whether natural, built or a combination of the two ... These physical symbols can be discovered in landscape features.'[12]

Erratics near Casla. Erratics are boulder glacial deposits from the retreat of the last Ice Age.

The glacial boulders, while obvious on land present considerable hazards to boats when they lurk just under the water's surface not familiar with the area.

Near Spiddal.

Changing wall-building practices. Traditional dry-stone walls sit against a recent garden wall. A renewed interest in traditional craft (including dry-stone wall building) has seen courses spring up around the country.

Death of Goll from Omey Island. Following his defeat at the hand of
Fionn the one fiery eye of Goll sinks into the sea.

Goll's Eye near Leenaun.

Looking to Hy-Brâzil. Hy-Brâzil was the land of the dead reached when spirits walked the Mag Mel. It was known by a multitude of names. Local belief in Hy-Brâzil was so strong and certain that it was given co-ordinates on John Purdy's first maritime map of Ireland in 1835. It was removed in 1860 revision although local belief persisted until the early twentieth century.

Evening sun reflections, Leenaun Pier.

Mass Rock south of Clifden.

Previous page:
Clifden, capital of Connemara.

Mag Mel and the death of Goll.

CHRISTIANITY AND INVASION

Many argue that Christianity did not arrive with Patrick, but instead was brought here by Palladius who was sent here by Pope Celestine I in 431.[1] Patrick was born the year after Palladius's mission and was, it seems, a little bit more of a showman than his forerunner when he banished the snakes and toads while his forgotten predecessor had concerned himself with the thankless task of converting pagans and saving souls. Consequently, we remember the singer and not the songwriter.

Regardless of who was responsible, Christianity's best way to win over the Irish was to assimilate traditions, euhemerise some gods and relegate others to the status of fairies.[2] Holy wells had many powerful associations with pre-Christian deities. Hazel trees grew around a large well in the centre of Hy-Brâzil.[3] The nuts that fell from the trees resurfaced as 'bubbles of knowledge' in rivers and wells around Ireland. These wells therefore held powerful healing properties and an important place within the inhabitants' beliefs. By ascribing Saints to the wells, Christianity was able to impose its belief system without directly confronting that of the natives. It is also not a coincidence that the cross of Brigid, who was previously a fire goddess, hangs above the hearth in Irish homes. Burial chambers where the gods and the dead resided were reduced to aes síde (people of the mound) or fairies.[4] Fairies, as we have been taught, are not to be trusted.

As the age of Conn, Goll and Fionn gave way to Christianity the new missionary colonisers instigated the aforementioned policy of cultural divide and conquer. Fairy folk would sour milk, steal babies, and kill cattle, amongst other pranks. To cajole the Irish into separating from their past was a sure way for Christianity to usurp previous faiths and to consolidate their own position.

The next two stories illustrate the menace of fairies. The first emphasises the importance of keeping to the Christian faith and not listening to your own voice. The following has many sources as with most Irish stories; that is their richness.

THE MASS ROCK

There was a time when priests were not always to be found, as the King of England did not want the faith practiced in Ireland. A young man, having spent a long day cutting turf in the bog just south of Clifden, returned home as satisfied with his day's labours as he was tired of them. No sooner had he sat down in his chair by the hearth than he fell into the deepest sleep that no wind would have shaken him from. During the night, as the embers burnt low, he did not stir but dreamt that a Mass was to be held at a large rock in a dip between two hills the next Sunday.

In the morning he woke feeling as ready for the day as he ever had. He put down his full rest to the good fortune of the dream. The

St Roc's Pass. The pass was cut as the Devil pulled the chain he had fastened around St Roc over the hill. The chain snapped after a struggle of forty days and nights.

young man knew the place he had dreamt of and the rock very well. All week he could think of nothing else but the Mass as he went about his work. Because of his preoccupation with the dream the week passed as quickly as a summer's night.

When the Sunday came around he polished his boots and got himself ready to set out for the Mass. As he approached the dip he could hear the murmur of the crowd as they waited for the Mass to begin. When he saw the congregation all the people looked new and strange to him. Not wanting to interrupt proceedings the young man stood at the back of the crowd waiting for the priest to begin. He didn't recognise the priest either and several times the priest caught the young man's eye. After the Mass the crowd left as quickly as he had come upon them and no one was left save himself and the priest.

'Seeing as how he acknowledged me during the Mass', thought the young man to himself, 'I should wait for him to talk to me.'

The priest approached the young man and said, 'How did you hear of this Mass?'

'I saw it in a dream', said the young man.

'In future,' said the priest, 'pay no attention to your dreams. We are not of your people. Do not come here again.'

I heard the following story in the Galway. There is a variant of the following story in Sean O'Sullivan's *Folktales of Ireland* (University of Chicago Press: Chicago, 1968). The source of O'Sullivan's version is also from Galway. The chapter it appears in is 'People of the Otherworld', the title of which again illustrates the distance Christianity wished to put between itself and past worship. It is interesting that the language of subtle prejudice is still in use in a contemporary publication.

Many Irish storytellers had their own signature of phrases which created their style. It could be a particular way of opening a story

Hidden Holy Well, Aill na Chapaill above Killary. Somewhere in the above panorama is a holy well. After hunting it for an afternoon the well decided to remain hidden. Rediscovering heritage is riddled with many such frustrations.

or a refrain that was used at intervals throughout the recitation, Such as, 'There was a time long ago, and it's long ago it was. If I'd been there then I wouldn't be here now. I'd have a new story or an old story or I'd be a grey-haired old storyteller. In any case, however well-off I am tonight, may ye not be half so well-off tomorrow night.' Through these signatures the lineage of a story can be traced.

THE WELL-DRESSED HORSEMAN

There was a young woman who lived between Clifden and Maam cross. Every year at the end of October a horse fair was held at Maam which lasted several days. People came from all over the parish and further for the fair, which was followed by dancing at night. One year, on the eve of the first day of the fair a well-dressed gentleman rode up to the house and dismounted his horse. The sun was beating strongly as he knocked on the door. The young woman who was cleaning within stopped her sweeping and went to answer the door.

'May I trouble you for a drink of water?' said the gentleman politely, 'Half the dust from the road is in my throat.'

'Sit down here on this stool,' the young woman replied, 'and I will fetch you some.'

The gentleman sat down on the stool by the door in the sun to mop his brow with a handkerchief. The woman returned with a cup and jug of water and set it down beside him so that he could have his fill. Parched with the exertions of his journey, the man hurriedly put his handkerchief back in the breast pocket of his jacket without much care so that he could quickly quench his thirst. He drank and drank until he had emptied the jug, whereupon he thanked the woman and left for the fair.

After he left she picked up the jug and cup and noticed that his handkerchief had fallen out of his pocket. 'Perhaps I can return it to him tomorrow at the fair when I go myself', she thought. She put it in her apron pocket and went inside. Eager to finish the housework so that she could be ready for the fair, she neglected to scatter used tea leaves before sweeping to prevent dust from rising. Some dust rose up and got into her right eye. She reached for the handkerchief

and made a point out of one corner so that she could get the speck. When she did she put the handkerchief back in her pocket.

The next day she got to the fair early and she saw more people at it than she had ever seen at a previous fair. Many of these people she had never seen before and they could not be seen by others. If she had rubbed the handkerchief in both eyes there is no telling what she would have been able to see.

She spent a happy time walking around the fair talking to those she knew and observing those she didn't, until eventually she saw the gentleman she had given the water to. With the handkerchief in her hand she went up to him and said, 'Here you are. You left your handkerchief at my house yesterday.'

He took it. 'How do you see me?' said he.

'I see you with my right eye.'

'Well then, you will see me no more', he replied.

He stuck a stick in her eye and pulled it out. And from that day until she died she had only one eye.

ST ROC AND THE DEVIL'S CHAIN

The origins of St Roc are uncertain but most sources say he was a devout local. Tim Robinson suggests that he may have been St Patrick's nephew St Ríoch.[5] Why the Devil should have picked on St Roc over other holy men I am not sure. He was not known to be a missionary with influence over conversions and did not have legions of committed followers. Perhaps the Devil liked serpents and bore a grudge against Patrick's nearest relative. His enduring legacy is a nearby holy well and a chapel at Salroc graveyard. In any case, the Devil was determined to win this seemingly incorruptible mystic. Perhaps that was the challenge. As St Roc was sleeping outside the village of Foher the Devil slipped a chain around his waist and locked it. As the Devil was crossing the ridge that separated Little Killary from Killary Harbour St Roc woke up. A struggle ensued for forty days and nights, with the Devil on one side of the ridge and Roc on the other. The struggle was so fierce that the ridge was cut in two. The chain became so fatigued after the weeks of rubbing that it snapped and Roc was freed.

Maam Ean and St Patrick's well.

The pass is in fact a fault in the bedrock and Killary Harbour is Ireland's only true fjord. On the summit at St Roc's pass are some stone daises which were used to rest coffins on as they were carried from Foher to Salroc graveyard. Coffins were not to touch the ground.

Foher itself suffered the devastation of many famine villages and now consists of no more than the shells of a few cottages. On the far side of the fjord is the remnants of another famine village, Uggool.[6] These two neighbouring villages show how densely populated this area once was. Marked on several maps above Foher on Aill na Chapaill (Cliff of the Horse) is a holy well. Despite being armed with two maps and an afternoon hunting I could not find it. This served as a reminder that 'The map is not the territory.'

MAAM EAN

Surrounded by a cloud of piranha midges is St Patrick's well at Maam Ean. The last Sunday of July every year sees a pilgrimage travel up the side of the mountain to perform a stations of the cross. This act of devotion is yet another example where Christianity has usurped a pagan tradition. The view from the well and small church built there is spectacular and to be savoured for as long as you can stand the flying carnivores savouring you.

OMEY ISLAND, ST FECHIN'S WELL AND AN EARLY CHRISTIAN GRAVEYARD.

Omey Island is a joy. The island is tidal and has no causeway so travelling to it needs to be planned and is an act of commitment.

Omey has evidence of some of Ireland's earliest settlements. The oldest signs of habitation here are the Mesolithic[7] shell middens (mid-Stone-Age rubbish tips). Most prehistoric settlement has been washed away by the sea and the same is now happening to the early Christian men's graveyard on the north coast at Trá na nÉan (Beach of the Birds). Bleached and yellowed bones, the same colour as the surrounding sands, are now being teased out of the dunes by the gentle but persistent lapping of the tide.

St Fechin was said to have had an early Christian settlement here. On the east side of the island tucked into the north side of a small bay is St Fechin's well, which is still visited by local devotees. The Christian claim to the well dates to the seventh century[8] but it possibly had pagan origins as a healing well before that. In contrast to the graveyard, St Fechin's church was buried by blown sands until it was excavated in 1981. It is a stone's throw away from the well.

THE FIRST HISTORY OF IRELAND

Just as Vasari's bias in his *Lives of the Artists* set the seat of the renaissance in his native town of Florence, Geraldus Cambrensis's (1146-1223) *The History and Topography of Ireland* (1185) influenced generations of historians to come and had echoes reflected in subsequent centuries. This has been much to the dismay of the Irish, who objected to being described as 'so barbarous that they cannot be said to have any culture'.[9] But that was probably a compliment given what was to follow, 'given only to pleasure, and devoted to laziness, they think the greatest pleasure is not to work'.[10] The final nail in the coffin was the description of their random acts of impulsive violence, 'From an old and evil custom they always carry an axe in their hand as if it were a staff. In this way, if they have a feeling for any evil, they can the more quickly give it effect.'[11] So there we have it, an unholy trinity of barbarity, sloth and evil. He goes on to criticise the existing clergy for letting their faith down.

No wonder these poor souls were in need of some new Christian salvation. Enter Christian Normans stage east.

Despite the quibbles the Irish may have had with Gerald of Wales's character assassination of them, his book is still the most important source of understanding of Ireland in the Middle Ages. If we can sift through the chaff of his prejudice and hearsay, and keep his own observations, the book has a lot to teach us. In any case, he does throw in the one compliment, 'It is only in the case of musical instruments that I find any commendable diligence in the people.'[12] Still, he claims, musically, the Irish are only second best to the Scottish and consequently, do not excel at anything.

Some solace can be taken from his praise for the island itself, which seems inversely proportional to his writings on its citizens. He comments on the great variety of flora and fauna in Ireland and acknowledges the lack of poisonous reptiles. He dismisses their banishment by St Patrick and instead claims it is because the air is so pure that as soon as venomous creatures touch the Irish soil they die. Because of the purity of the landscape, Ireland has no need for doctors, Gerald remarks, and the further west you go the healthier the air becomes. Today this still holds true; while the east is touched by the air of nuclear reactors and has the greatest density of industry, it is the lack of industry in the west that caused so many to emigrate and has kept the air and sea amongst the cleanest in Europe.

Gerald is pretty singular in his praise of the west over the east, 'the advantages of the west outshine and outstrip those of the east'.[13] But then he did not have to earn a living there. I suppose in the Normans' eyes Gerald's published overview of a beautiful land populated with lazy reprobates confirmed it was a country worth invading.

FROM NORMAN TO NOW

The next few centuries saw the end of society's Brehon structure.[14] This enlightened legal system was replaced with Norman law and a feudal structure. By this time paganism had all but been replaced by Christianity.

The soil of the west was notoriously difficult to farm. It suffered from the double blows of being very boggy and very stony. The glacial stone strewn over the fields was cleared to make walls. Every now and then an opening in the walls was filled with a looser stack of rocks to create stone gates in order to allow the movement of animals between one field and another.

The animals contained within the walls also take their place within the stories and lore of Ireland. Probably the most famous Irish legend of all is the Cattle Raid of Cooley (Táin Bó Cúailnge). Usually referred to as *The Táin*. This story has spurned many interpretations across a variety of arts, including the seminal translation by Thomas Kinsella with illustrations by Louis le Brocquy and a recent powerful translation by Ciaran Carson. In 1973 Horselips brought out an electric (and I'm not just referring to the instruments) album called *The Táin*. This once more became a nation's battle cry as Jack's army replaced Cú Chulainn's in 'Italia '90' and 'Dearg Doom' sounded across the country when we enjoyed our first and still our best World Cup finals. Macnas put on a mesmerising performance of *The Táin* during the Galway Arts Festival in 1992.

Cattle have been an important part of the fabric of the Irish economy and society since 3500 BC.[15] In *The Táin* the brown bull (Donn) shares its name with the god of the dead.[16] While white cows are thought to be related to those brought to Britain by the Romans.[17] These white red-eared cows also hold a strong place in Irish legend. Morrígan disguises herself as one when she attacks Cú Chulainn.[18] White cows in early literature were thought to be particularly valuable but through the years they became associated with bad luck as they were coveted by fairies more than any other colour. Consequently white cows in a herd were thought to be unlucky. Farmers went to great lengths to keep fairy folk away from their herd. Just as pagan cultures would make offerings to gods, farmers would throw a measure of the first of the milk into the air for the fairies. If you visit the holy wells of Ireland it is quickly apparent that this tradition of offering to gods is still strong. However, now the god is Christian.

While cattle may have been the most valuable livestock by a country mile, sheep were by far the most numerous. Their absence in Irish folkore reflects their lower economic value. It was believed if you were to peer through the shoulder blade from a sheep's skeleton you could see into the future.[19] If you want to try this for yourself Connemara is littered with the carcasses of sheep snared by bog holes and ravaged by dogs. It should be pretty easy to find a shoulder blade.

No animal is more associated with Connemara than the Connemara pony. Remains of domesticated horses have been dated from 2000 BC. Early histories claim that horses were brought to Ireland by Lugh, a god of continental Celtic origin. Horses were revered animals and to eat their flesh was forbidden. The Connemara pony is probably a mix of an early Irish breed and foreign stock. The exalted status of the horse is paralleled with their spiritual significance. Horses carried men between here and the Otherworld just as Oisín returned from Tír na nÓg on the back of a white horse. Horses could also see ghosts and fairies. There is another story demonstrating horses' ability to pass between one world and another.

Apart from a decent crop of stones, the wet soil did not lend itself well to many other crops. One which did find favour was the potato. Potatoes combined with fishing provided the bulk of the diet for those living on the coast. But all this changed in 1845 when the first year of the famine rotted the harvest in the ground. More recently, subsistence fishing has not been sustainable as a way of life. Traditional fishing has been replaced by larger trawlers and farms.

The industrial revolution that started a few decades before the famine acted as a lure, pulling the starving Irish further west to their Hy-Brâzil on Coney Island. The scale of the depopulation is easily seen in the number of crumbling stone cottages. The gentle corrugations of lazy beds and the occasional famine village underscore the devastation visited on the population. This movement away from Connemara continued in waves over the next century but never revisited the intensity of the years following the famine. In the 1950s and 1960s much of the movement was to the construction sites of London.

THE WATER HORSE

A farmer from the foothills of Erris Beg out cutting turf saw a horse rise up out of a bog lake. He grabbed a rope and soon calmed and caught the horse. The horse had never been sick for a day and was the strongest and swiftest he had ever seen. But even the most diligent and hardworking will tire. After a long sweltering summer's day bringing seaweed from the beach to a field, the horse stumbled and the cart almost tipped over on the uneven path. The farmer then gave the horse a flick of the whip, where upon it broke loose from the reigns and disappeared into the pool from which it had come. The next day the farmer grew sick and died a short time later.

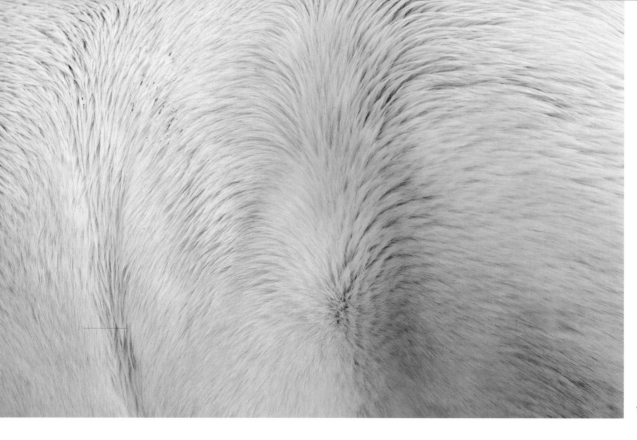

White pony at Maam Cross Pony Fair.

Black pony at Maam Cross Pony Fair.

Selling ponies, Maam Cross Pony Fair.

Bog Walk, Maam Cross.

Buyers and sellers on the first day at Maam Cross Pony Fair.

Foher and Fish farm. The Connemara landscape is full of lines, the buoys of the fish farm, field walls, lazy beds, drying turf, roads and their markings. Sometimes the terrain feels more like an exercise in the aesthetics of geometry than the soft organic topography we have come to expect.

St Fechin's well, Omey.

Early Christian Graveyard, Omey. Men's graveyard on bird beach.

St Fechin's well had pre-Christian healing associations and became Christian in the sixth and seventh centuries.

Omey.

Lichens and crab leg. Omey Island.

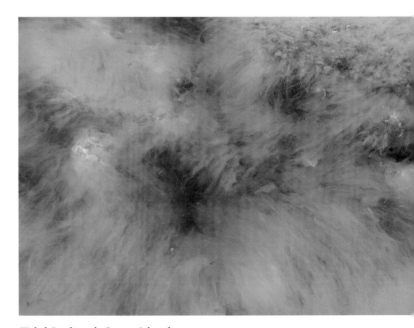

Crab remains as a seagull. Omey Island.

Tidal Rockpool. Omey Island.

Looking from Omey to Cruagh.

Fingers written by Erosion. Omey Island.

Omey Lichens. Looking towards Cruach. Gerald of Wales said that the Irish had no need for doctors as the air and land was so pure and that the further west you travelled the purer they became.

Omey Lichens. Looking Towards Hy-Brâzil.

*Sheep and turf
wall at the back of
Errisbeg.*

Stone wall.

Wall and roof.

Stone wall at the foot of Errisbeg.

Near Fermoyle. The perpetual wheels of development, as stone is quarried from one field to be relocated and built in another.

Cottage at famine village near Carna.

Stone wall and tide.

Stone wall at famine village near Carna.

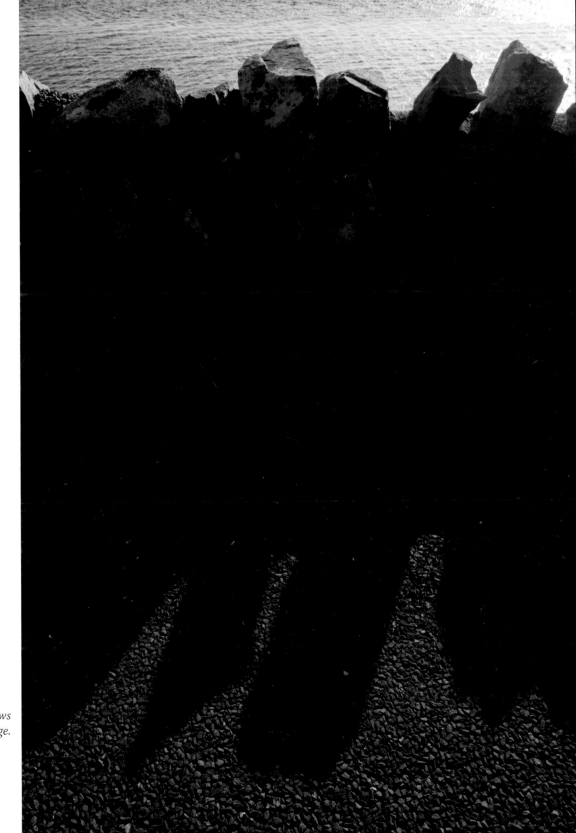

Seafront stone wall casting crooked teeth shadows across the road near Pearse's Cottage.

Sheep at the back of Errisbeg.

Cows near Carna.

Sheep on bog wall.

Sheep and statue.

Connemara Pony, Roundstone.

The Connemara Pony has associations with the work pony described in the 'Crith Gablach'. These horses have a connection with the Celtic inhabitants of Ireland.

Broken boat and lazy beds, Killary.

Broken boat and grasses, Killary. Small-scale subsistence fishing has given way to efficient larger trawlers and national industries.

Roundstone Bog and the Twelve Bens.

Famine Village near Carna.

Foher.

Garden Fork, famine village, near Carna.

Breeched wall in famine village near Carna.

Walls, Spiddal.

Cottage on the road to Leitir Mór. The Leitir Mór area is one of the strongest Irish-speaking regions in Connemara.

Broken door on ground, famine village, near Carna.

Bog stream and glacial deposits, Casla.

Bog Road Bend, south of the Casla—Ros an Mhíl crossroad.

Trees, Spiddal.

Sign, Recess.

Turf walls and Twelve Bens. Turf walls are at once an example of tradition and trust. The turf needs to dry and the airy walls help this. Turf theft from unattended walls is not uncommon.

Stools on the Twelve Bens.

Cloudscape.

Cloud shadow, mountains and coniferous forest.

Killary Fjord at the close of day from the Victorian Jetty in Leenaun.

THE AGE OF SCIENCE AND SECULARISM

Clifden, the capital of Connemara, was cut off from the rest of the island except by a few bog tracks until Alexander Nimmo completed the Galway–Clifden road in 1835,[1] just in time for the droves to leave a decade later.

Apart from the lure of opportunity the industrial revolution presented it also heralded the 'Age of Steam'. This represented the first real attempt to create a network of mass transport, which has reached its current peak with budget air travel. In 1891 work started on the Galway–Clifden railway with the intention of stimulating the fishing industry. However the decision to route it inland undermined this, as all the fishing villages bar Clifden were bypassed. Having failed to meet its initial objectives, the line attempted to attract tourism to the west but this was not enough to sustain it. The line was completed with enormous expense in 1895 and closed forty years later. During the four decades the railway was operational, it opened Connemara up to tourism and helped to establish sea fisheries, providing a much-needed economic stimulus to the region. Remnants of Connemara's most costly infrastructure project can still be seen if you follow the track through the central plain. It can be seen how the track is punctuated with bridges as it snakes along its raised bed. Of course Clifden is much more accessible today because of cars. Aer Arann also plays its role in helping to keep the islands connected to the mainland.

The late twentieth century saw a different type of depopulation. Church vocations and congregations all over the island are shrinking. This is in part due to recent Church scandals and a growing disinterest in established religions, as seen through the rise of secular marriages and multi-denominational schools. It is also a consequence of the continued draw of urban work, as the land can support fewer of the people it produces. Graveyards are now tended to by ferns and sheep while cobwebs sit on the bell which used to call to the distant faithful. Combined with a new alter at the tills of consumerism during the years of economic boom have also had their taken their toll.

The increased mechanisation of previously labour-intensive industries has provided a few with a livelihood where once the same industry would have been divided amongst more workers. Turf cutting and fish farming are good examples of this. Production of turf (a high CO_2 emitting fuel) is under threat as government policy changes Bord na Mona's role from fuel production to bog conservation. As fewer people remain to support local businesses, they too suffer, and pubs and shops close.

Coniferous forests, whose pine-green foliage covered the landscape in a discoloured acidic rash, is in part being removed so that once more the blanket bogs will have a chance to establish themselves. This is a very welcome state policy. It is ironic that the blanket bogs only established themselves as a consequence of prehistoric deforestation.

The quietness and solitude of Connemara that drove away younger generations seeking opportunity is the very thing that

Mechanical turf cuts near Maam Ean.

now draws tourists. Tourism, if managed correctly, has a real chance of supporting the local population. Development needs to be approached with care. The ribbons of the last decade's holiday homes and a manicured experience of the landscape only serve to lessen the impressiveness of the unspoilt landscape which is now all too rare in Europe.

The plethora of tax-break hotels have taken valuable bed-nights from B&Bs, thereby increasing the number of day trippers from Galway and further removing the value of tourism to the local economy. Even the visitors to the holiday homes stock up at their local supermarket before they travel west, fearing they won't be able to get the anchovies and capers they need. If we want to find things the same as we always have had them why do we bother to leave home in the first place? The local economy needs to be supported if we want it to be there the next time.

Perhaps the most obvious sign of visitors' lack of understanding of the local landscape are the seemingly infinite number of 'NO DOGS' signs. Without this basic understanding the farmer has to deal with the savage consequences.

For such an unspoilt landscape it is surprising to find Connemara covered in lines almost anywhere you look. Once you notice them and discover the way they echo and call each other they begin to seamlessly fit together. They remind us of far more self-conscious attempts to tame the landscape by land artists such as Robert Smithson and Andy Goldsworthy. Here, the natural ebb and flow of placement and removal have created an effortless poetry that is almost impossible to purposefully recreate.

Nimmo's Jetty, Roundstone.

Roundstone.

Galway—Clifden Railway crossing
Abhainn Mór at the Cluan Beg Bridge.

Galway—Clifden Railway at the Cluan
Beg Bridge. While the age of steam is full
of romantic associations many parts of
the route are impassable and present very
real dangers.

Galway–Clifden Railway crossing Abhainn Tua near Recess.

Aer Arann. Where the state railway failed to provide a lasting connection for remote regions subsidised private industry is now attempting to fill the void.

Roundstone. Cloch an Rón, stone of the seals, built by Alexander
Nimmo between 1822 and 1825. Its annual regatta of Galway Hookers is
a big tourist attraction.

Church bell with cobweb at Béal an Átha Fada.

Ferns and graves at Béal an Átha Fada.

Lobster pots on Nimmo's Jetty at Roundstone.

Fish farm in Killary Fjord.

Mweelrea Mountains and fish farm.

Coniferous stumps, Binn Gabhar.

Blanket bog rejuvenation, Tievebreen.

Bog hole, Binn Gabhar.

Forest clearance near Maam Cross.

Post-clearance, remaining trunks,
Tievebreen.

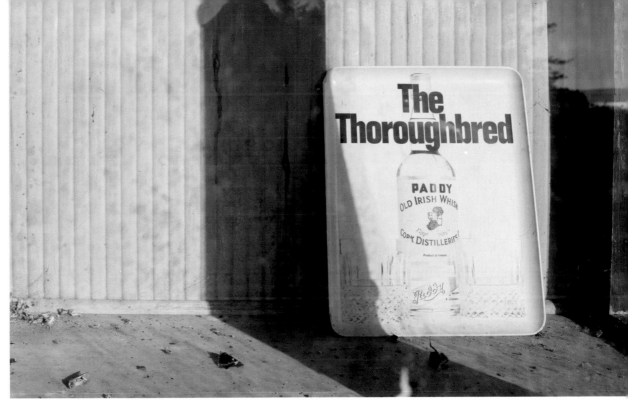

Shop and pub window.

Deserted pub.

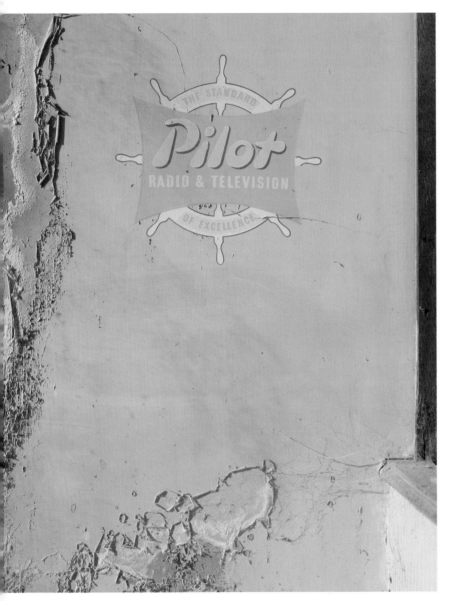

Pilot radio and television on pub wall.

Closed pub outside Spiddal.

No dogs, south of Clifden.

Gate at Maam Ean with no dogs sign.

No dogs, Killary Fjord.

Sheep and bog hole on Roundstone bog.

Wall and carcass above Killary Fjord.

Fish farm after Robert Smithson, land artist.

Turf lines, Recess.

Stone-walled fields.

Echo Errisbeg.

*Pylons. Brooding clouds hover over electricity sub-station at Athry on
the road from Clifden.*

Previous Page:
Rhododendron and Cottage. Rhododendron introduced by the Victorians as part of the managed landscape creeps up the back of the hill on a deserted cottage.

Killary Walk.

Twelve Bens and turf wall. Sometimes forms built to respond to the landscape seem very self-conscious. At other times they feel part of a more organic and instinctual process. Finding examples of this empathy is a joy.

Killary Fjord.

Bog lake.

Leenaun from the Victorian jetty.

Bog cutting on Roundstone bog.

Fishing at Killary Fjord.

Maam Cross.

From Errisbeg.

Grasses.

CONCLUSION

We are experiencing a growing disconnect with the culture of our landscape. Landscape has more than a purely aesthetic or commercial function. Tibor Kalman said, 'I have nothing against beauty, I just find it boring.' If beauty is to have any role at all, it must co-exist with something else to give it meaning. The land has a role as a depository for our collective memory and culture and that is what this book has attempted to uncover. I have tried to draw attention to the ephemeral nature of our landscape and to the way in which we steer its evolution, just as it has evolved us.

The direction of that evolution is a choice we can make. Change can take a long time to have effect. The new policy of removing state coniferous forest to grow back the blanket bog is a good example. Another co-existence needs to be acknowledged, that of the land and its inhabitants. Controversies surrounding fish farms and the concerns of protestors in Rossport draw attention to this. The relationship needs to be symbiotic if it is to be sustainable. Anything else is short term. Respecting the non-commercial function in a commercial world is the problem we have to balance.

Despite Connemara's remoteness, it has not been immune to the effects of time and civilisation. This book has attempted to examine the interplay between the landscape and those it has supported; how the land inspired our culture and how in response culture has left its marks on the land. These tracks have become increasingly brutal of late; made for the benefit of commerce and development. It is important to rediscover the more subtle but profound relationship that we once had with the space we inhabited, to refrain from solely placing a price tag on our surroundings, but to see the richer gifts it has to offer.

Quarry, outside Clifden.

EPILOGUE: WHY WE CAME TO BE HERE

Standing in the middle of seeming Nowhere
Looking in all directions and beyond the horizon
Further than the compass and eye can see
A being here, being alone and feeling first
Until seeing in all directions and beyond the horizon
Further than the compass and eye can see
Artefacts of yesterday and everyday

Trees at Maam Cross. Trees are bent in the direction of the prevailing wind.

Pine copse.

Closed quarry gate, outside Clifden. The easy rhythmic formal lines of the quarry's fence contrasts with its more aggressive daily function.

Planted conifers on the foothills of Maam Ean.

BIBLIOGRAPHY AND ENDNOTES

Bruce, N., (Director) *I Could Read the Sky*

Chatwin, B., *The Songlines* (Penguin: London, 1988).

Dames, M., *Mythic Ireland* (Thames & Hudson: London, 1996). P.167.

Dillon, M., *There was a King in Ireland* (University of Texas: San Antonio, 1971).

Herman, D., *Great Walks of Ireland* (Hodder Headline: London, 1999). P.102.

Kelly, F., *Early Irish Farming* (Dublin Institute for Advanced Studies: Dublin, 1997). P.30.

Kelly, F., *Early Irish Law* (Dublin Institute for Advanced Studies: Dublin, 1988).

La Farge, O., *The American Indian* (Golden Press: New York, 1972).

MacCuloch, J.A., *Celtic Mythology* (Dover Publications: New York, 2004). P.20.

Madden, F.J.M., *The History of Ireland* (Hodder Education: London, 2005). P.5.

O'Grady, T. & Pyke, S., *I Could Read The Sky* (Random House: London, 1997).

Ó hÓgáin, D., *The Lore of Ireland* (The Collins Press: Cork, 2006). P.279.

Ó'Lionáird, I., *I Could Read the Sky* (Real World Records, 2002)

O'Meara, J., (trans) Gerald of Wales, *The History and Topography of Ireland.* (Penguin Books: London, 1982).

Rackard, A., & O'Callaghan, L., *Fish Stone Water* (Attic Press: Cork, 2002).

Robinson, T., *Connemara: Introduction and Gazetteer* (Folding Landscapes: Roundstone, 2005).

Robinson, T., *Setting foot on the Shores of Connemara* (Lilliput: Dublin, 1996). P.5.

Robinson, T., ed. Aalen, Whelan & Stout, *Atlas of the Rural Irish Landscape* (Cork University Press: Cork, 1997).

Smyth, D., *A Guide to Irish Mythology* (Irish Academic Press: Dublin, 1996). P.83.

ENDNOTES

INTRODUCTION

1. Robinson, T., ed. Aalen, Whelan & Stout, *Atlas of the Rural Irish Landscape* (Cork University Press: Cork, 1997).
2. Cato & Bridgeman, *One Giant Leap*, Palm Pictures.
3. Chatwin, B., *The Songlines* (Penguin: London, 1988).
4. La Farge, O., *The American Indian* (Golden Press: New York, 1972).
5. Dames, M., *Mythic Ireland* (Thames & Hudson: London, 1996). P.167.
6. Dames.
7. *ibid.*
8. Conversation with Dr Eamon Slater, NUI, Maynooth.
9. Dames.
10. O'Grady, T. & Pyke, S., *I Could Read The Sky* (Random House: London, 1997).
11. Rackard, A., & O'Callaghan, L., *Fish Stone Water* (Attic Press: Cork, 2002).
12. Robinson, T., *Setting on the shores of Connemara* (Lilliput: Dublin, 1996).

BEFORE WORDS WERE WRITTEN

1. O'Connell, M., *Connemara* (OPW: Dublin, 1994). P.12.
2. Robinson, T., *Stepping on the Shores of Connemara* (Lilliput: Dublin, 1996). P.5.
3. Dames. P.157.
4. Smyth, D., *A Guide to Irish Mythology* (Irish Academic Press: Dublin, 1996). P.83.
5. Smyth. P.65.
6. Ó hÓgáin, D., *The Lore of Ireland* (The Collins Press: Cork, 2006). P.279.
7. Dames. P.164.
8. Smyth. P.38.
9. Dames. P.166.
10. Smyth. P.144.
11. MacCuloch, J.A., *Celtic Mythology* (Dover Publications: New York, 2004). P.20.
12. Dames. P.14.

CHRISTIANITY AND INVASION

1. Madden, F.J.M., *The History of Ireland* (Hodder Education: London, 2005). P.5.
2. MacCuloch. P.18.
3. Dames. P.170.
4. Dames. P.12.

5. Robinson, T., *Connemara: Introduction and Gazetteer* (Folding Landscapes: Roundstone, 2005). P.32.
6. Herman, D., *Great Walks of Ireland* (Hodder Headline: London, 1999). P.102.
7. Robinson, T., ed. Aalen, Whelan & Stout. P.332.
8. Rackard, A., & O'Callaghan, L. P.104.
9. O'Meara, J., (trans) Gerald of Wales, *The History and Topography of Ireland* (Penguin Books: London, 1982). P.101.
10. O'Meara. P.102.
11. O'Meara. P.107.
12. O'Meara. P.103.
13. O'Meara. P.56.
14. Kelly, F., *Early Irish Law* (Dublin Institute for Advanced Studies: Dublin, 1997).
15. Kelly, F., *Early Irish Farming* (Dublin Institute for Advanced Studies: Dublin, 1997). P.30.
16. Horselips *The Táin* (Release Records: Dublin, 1973). LP sleeve notes.
17. Ó hÓgáin. P.71.
18. Kelly, F., *Early Irish Farming*. P.33.
19. Ó hÓgáin. P.454

THE AGE OF SCIENCE AND SECULARISM

1. Robinson, T., ed. Aalen, Whelan & Stout. P.338.

TECHNICAL INFORMATION

EQUIPMENT

EOS 1DsIII
Canon and Hartblei lenses
Manfrotto Panoramic Head
VW Camper.

PROCESSING

Photoshop CS3 and CS4
Hugin 0.8 (http://hugin.sourceforge.net) It's open source, so if you like it do the right thing and make a donation.